Let's Join in!

compiled by Christine Wright

illustrated by Eira Reeves

Scripture Union
130 City Road, London EC1V 2NJ

Foreword

'Let's Join In' is a collection of songs and rhymes which aims to get children and adults taking an active part in learning about and worshipping God.

The items have been chosen with children up to eight years old in mind, with some which are especially for pre-school children. An important feature of 'Let's Join In' is that many items could be used with a much wider age-range, in all-age worship, for instance. There are some suggestions in the index, but, as each church is unique, leaders may find others in this collection that all generations can enjoy together.

I hope, above all, that people will have fun using this book and that it will encourage people of all ages, learning and worshipping together, to discover the delight of joining in.

Christine Wright

Authors

Pat Baker
Liz Baker
Valerie Clements
Sheila Clift
Kathleen Crawford
Hazel Elsworthy
Kathleen Fennell
Sally Fox
Dilys Gower

Dorothy Higgins
Elizabeth Hume
Peggy Jackson
Cecilia King
Jill McWilliam
Elsie Newman
Margaret Old
Christine Orme
Chris Powell

Sharon Ralph
Heather Rodman
Susan Ryan
Margaret Shearer
Jacqui Sibley
Joan Stride
Jean Watson
Rose Williams
Christine Wright

British Library Cataloguing in Publication Data
Let's join in!: a collection of action songs and rhymes.
1. Children's action songs in English
I. Wright, Christine   II. Reeves Eira
784.6'24'00942

© Scripture Union 1990

First published 1990
Reprinted 1992

Designed by Sue Ainley

ISBN 0 86201 622 3

Phototypeset by Input Typesetting Ltd, London

Music setting by Halstan & Co. Ltd., Amersham, Bucks

Printed and bound in Great Britain at The Bath Press, Avon

Contents

Acknowledgements

Most of the items in this book were previously published in Scripture Union 'Learning Together with Under-5s' (and its predecessor 'Teaching Under-5s') and other 'Learning Together' magazines. Where known, the authors' names are listed opposite. My thanks to all of them and to Kathleen Crawford, Elsie Newman and Joan Stride who contributed new items. I apologise to any author whose work has not been credited. Please inform the publisher and this will be rectified in any future editions of 'Let's Join In'.

The Lord – and the Lord alone – is our God!

God is the one who tells us what to do.
He always knows what's best for me and you.
He helps us all in every way,
He is the one to follow every day.
The Lord – and the Lord alone – is our God!
Hold up left hand, then right hand, clap three times on last three syllables.
The Lord – and the Lord alone – is our God!
Repeat.

God is the King who rules above all.
He loves us all both big and small.
If we love him and keep his laws,
He'll take good care of us for ever more.
The Lord – and the Lord alone – is our God!
Actions as before.
The Lord – and the Lord alone – is our God!

(Based on Deuteronomy 6:4)

Busy hands

Mime actions with hands.

Gently, gently stroke the cat,
Tie a bow on baby's hat,
Take a sweet from Granny's tin,
Wipe the breadcrumbs from my chin,
Brush my teeth and blow my nose,
Fasten buttons on my clothes,
Cook the dinner, wash the pans,
Thank you, God, for two strong hands!
Hold out hands.

God loves me

This can be sung to the traditional tune, 'Three blind mice'.

God loves me,
I can see,
God loves me,
I can see
The trees, the birds and the sun that shines,
The houses, the buses, the railway lines.
I open my eyes and I see all the signs
That God loves me.

I will sing to the Lord

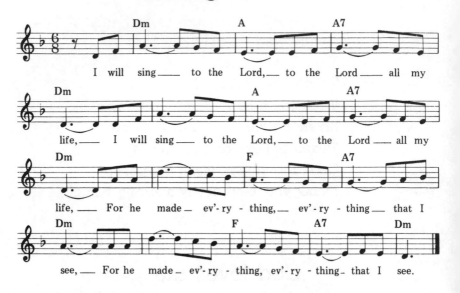

I will sing to the Lord, to the Lord all my life.
I will sing to the Lord, to the Lord all my life.
For he made everything, everything that I see.
For he made everything, everything that I see.

Actions: I will sing (*point to self*)
        to the Lord (*hands together*)
        all my life (*two claps*)
        for he made everything (*hands outstretched*)
        that I see (*hand above eye*)

Father God, you show your care

Leader: Father God, you show your care for the land by sending rain;
Mime, with fingers, rain falling.

You fill the streams with water;
Mime, with hands, water rushing along.

You provide the earth with crops of food;
Mime picking and eating of fruit.

This is how you do it;

You send abundant rain on the ploughed fields and soak them with water;
Clap with two fingers to make 'rain' noise.

You soften the soil with showers and cause the young plants to grow.
Mime growth by crouching down and 'growing' slowly.

What a rich harvest your goodness provides!
Everyone claps.

The pastures are filled with flocks of sheep; the hillsides are full of joy. The fields are covered with sheep.

Everyone shouts and sings for joy.
Everyone shouts, 'Thank you, Father God!'

(From Psalm 65:9–11)

God's our Father

This song can be sung as a call and response, a leader singing the first phrase and everyone else singing the repeat. With much older children and adults, it may be sung as a round.

God's our Father, God's our Father,
He gives life, he gives life.
He made the world around us,
He made the world around us.
Thank you, God, thank you, God.

God sent Jesus, God sent Jesus,
He's God's Son, he's God's Son.
He shows the Father loves us,
He shows the Father loves us.
Thank you, God, thank you God.

Holy Spirit, Holy Spirit,
He's from God, he's from God.
He helps us live like Jesus,
He helps us live like Jesus.
Thank you, God, thank you, God.

God the true God, God the true God,
He is Lord, he is Lord.
Father and Son and Spirit,
Father and Son and Spirit.
Thank you, God, thank you, God.

Be glad, earth and sky!

Be glad, earth and sky!
Raise both arms.
Roar, sea, and every creature in you;
Mime waves with arms.
Be glad, fields, and everything in you!
Raise both arms.
The trees in the woods will shout for joy when the Lord comes to rule the earth.
Shout for joy! Shout for joy! Shout for joy!

(From Psalm 96:11–13)

Praise God!

All: Praise God! Praise God!
Wave arms in praise.

Leader: For he made by his power,
This enormous world of ours.

All: We love you, God!
Thank you, God!
Arms outstretched.

All: Praise God! Praise God!
Wave arms in praise.

Leader: He gives us love and care,
Food to eat and clothes to wear.

All: We love you, God!
Thank you, God!
Arms outstretched.

All: Praise God! Praise God!
Wave arms in praise.

Leader: He has sent his dear Son,
With love for everyone.

All: We love you, God!
Thank you, God!
Arms outstretched.

Sing for joy

Leader: Sing for joy to the Lord, all the earth!

Response (everyone clapping or playing percussion):
            Sing for joy! Sing for joy!

Leader: Praise him with songs and shouts of joy!

Response: Sing for joy! Sing for joy!

Leader: Sing praise to the Lord!

Response: Sing for joy! Sing for joy!

Leader: Play on the harps! Blow trumpets and horns
            and shout for joy to the Lord our King.

Response: Sing for joy! Sing for joy!

Leader: Roar, sea, and every creature in you.

Response: Sing for joy! Sing for joy!

Leader: Clap your hands, you rivers.

Response: Sing for joy! Sing for joy!

Leader: You hills, sing together with joy before the
            Lord.

Response: Sing for joy! Sing for joy!

(From Psalm 98:4–8)

God made the grass

God made the grass, he made the trees,
Hold up fingers to form grass, then lift arms to form trees.
He made the sun that shines.
Draw circle in the air.
He made the mountains and the seas.
Draw curve which peaks high, then drops low.
Thank you, God, for these!

God made the butterflies and bees,
Hook thumbs together, wave fingers.
The horses, cats and dogs,
Mime stroking.
The fish, the birds, the chimpanzees.
Wriggle hands low, then high, scratch chest.
Thank you, God, for these!

God made you and God made me.
Point to others and self.
He made our eyes and ears,
Point to eyes and ears.
Our hands and feet, our heads and knees.
Point to parts of body.
Thank you, God, for these!

Thank you for the world you made

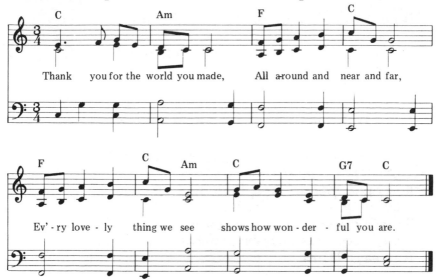

Thank you for the world you made,
All around and near and far.
Every lovely thing we see,
Shows how wonderful you are.

Raindrops on the window pane,
Streams and rivers flowing far.
Every lovely thing we see,
Shows how wonderful you are.

Clear blue sky and fluffy clouds,
Silvery moon and brightest star.
Every lovely thing we see,
Shows how wonderful you are.

Snowflakes, frost and icicles,
Part of your creation are.
Every lovely thing we see,
Shows how wonderful you are.

The sun

Here is the washing blowing on the line.
Flap hands.

Mummy pegs it out when the weather is fine.
Pretend to peg out clothes.

So let's clap our hands for the sun today
Clap three times and then point upwards with both hands.

And say, 'Thank you' to God when we stand to pray.

Down in the garden the buds start to swell,
Cup hands together to form a flower bud.

Red ones, yellow ones, blue ones as well.
Stretch fingers outwards like flower petals opening.

So let's clap our hands for the sun today
Clap three times then point upwards with both hands.

And say, 'Thank you' to God when we stand to pray.

Can you see the strawberries ripening in the sun?
Shade eyes with hand.

We'll have enough for tea if we pick every one.
Bend down and pretend to pick strawberries.

So let's clap our hands for the sun today
Clap three times and then point upwards with both hands.

And say, 'Thank you' to God when we stand to pray.

God provides

Pussycat, pussycat
Traditional tune

Ap - ples, po - ta - toes and fresh milk and cheese,
Food that is giv - en to us ev' - ry day. We
thank you our Fa - ther for your lov - ing care And
thank you for peo - ple who love us, we say.

Apples, potatoes and fresh milk and cheese;
Food that is given to us every day.
We thank you, our Father, for your loving care,
And thank you for people who love us, we say.

Trousers and dresses, warm jumpers and shoes;
Clothes that are given to us every day.
We thank you, our Father, for your loving care,
And thank you for people who love us, we say.

Houses to go to, with warm beds at night;
Safely we live in our homes every day.
We thank you, our Father, for your loving care,
And thank you for people who love us, we say.

15

Oh thank you!

Music: Elizabeth Hume

It's grow-ing ve - ry slow - ly. It's peep-ing thro' the ground. I see it in my gar - den, a yel - low daff - o - dil. Oh thank you, oh thank you for all the things you make. Oh thank you, oh thank you, Fa - ther God.

Here is a seed

This rhyme introduces the idea of the cycle of life and death, which is an important part of creation.

Here is a seed.
  Mime holding tiny seed.
Plant it in the ground.
  Mime planting.
From it grows a flower with petals all around.
  Wrists together, open hands.
After a while the flower must die,
  Curl fingers.
But you mustn't worry, you need not cry.
  Shake head.
Inside the flower where the petals used to be,
  Peer into 'flower'.
Look very carefully and you will see
Brand new seeds waiting to be found,
  Mime picking up seeds from one hand with the other.
Waiting to be planted back into the ground.
  Mime planting.

Today's surprise

When I wake up early in the morning,
I stretch and yawn and blink and rub my eyes,
Then tiptoe quickly over to the window
To see if I can see today's surprise!

It may be a lacy cobweb sparkling with dew
Or a robin redbreast sitting in a tree,
Some snowflakes or a raindrop running down the pane,
A rainbow or a busy bumble bee;

The sunlight painting colours on a flower
Or stars and moon that light the evening skies.
Thank you, God, for all your gifts and treasures
And for sending us each day a new surprise!

Plant the seeds

Music: Cliff Ince

1. Plant the seeds   Plant the seeds   In the ground   and   watch them as   they   grow.
2. Comes the wind   Comes the rain   Comes the   sun   In   time   the   seeds   will   grow.

Chorus

Grow-ing in-to veg'ta-bles good to eat. Grow-ing in-to flow'rs that smell so sweet. Grow-ing in-to food that we all need.

Thank you, God, for the ti-ny seed.

Seasons song

Music: Elizabeth Hume

Spring time— There will al-ways be spring time.

Spring time— There will al-ways be spring time. _____ A time for

clear-ing the weeds and a time for plant-ing the seeds. __

That's how— God said it would be. __

Spring time, there will always be spring time.
Spring time, there will always be spring time.
A time for clearing the weeds
And a time for planting the seeds.
That's how God said it would be.

Summer time, there will always be summer time.
Summer time, there will always be summer time.
A time when the work has been done
And a time for enjoying the sun.
That's how God said it would be.

Autumn time, there will always be autumn time.
Autumn time, there will always be autumn time.
The corn is ripening
And the farmers gather it in.
That's how God said it would be.

Winter time, there will always be winter time.
Winter time, there will always be winter time.
A time for ice and snow,
A time when the fires glow.
That's how God said it would be.

My body

I have a head with a mouth and a nose,
Hands on head; point to mouth and nose.

Ears and eyes – two each of those.
Touch ears and eyes, – hold up both forefingers.

I have arms with elbow bends,
Stretch arms out sideways at shoulder level, palms up; flex elbows.

And hands with fingers at each end.
Stretch arms out in front; waggle fingers.

Here is my tummy that holds all I eat.
Hands on tummy.

Here are my legs – and my knees – and my feet!
Touch thighs, knees, feet in turn.

This is my body – God made me –
Indicate head to toe with both hands; point to self.

I can jump and run, and hear and see,
Jump, run on spot, touch ears and eyes.

Thank you, God!

My hands and feet

Mime actions with hands.

What can I do with my hands?
I can hold a fork and spoon,
Brush my hair and draw the moon.
I can wave and I can clap!
I can gently stroke the cat.
Push and pull and things like that.
Thank you, God, for hands!

Mime actions with feet.

What can I do with my feet?
I can walk and I can run.
I can skip and have some fun.
I can hop and climb a tree.
I can paddle in the sea,
Stamp and jump and dance with glee!
Thank you, God, for feet!

Noah noise rhyme

Decide with children how to produce the noises in the rhyme, using percussion instruments or vocal sounds.

Bang, bang, bang
Went the hammer on the wood.
Noah built the ark
Because God said he should.

Roar, gobble, squeak
Went the animals together.
We'll be safe in here
No matter what the weather!

Splish, splash, splosh
Went the waves against the ark.
Noah and his family
Waited in the dark.

Crash, creak, groan
Went the ark against the ground.
They landed on a mountain
God had kept them safe and sound.

Nehemiah

Here are the walls of Jerusalem.
Hold up hands to form 'wall'.

Here are the stones that lay on the ground
Make fists like stones.
That became the walls of Jerusalem.

Here are the workers, strong and brave,
Make fingers stand straight.
Who lifted the stones that lay on the ground
That became the walls of Jerusalem.

Here is Nehemiah who prayed to God
Thumb alone.
To help the workers, strong and brave,
Who lifted the stones that lay on the ground
That became the walls of Jerusalem.

Here are the people who shouted and sang
Wriggle fingers.
With Nehemiah who prayed to God
To help the workers, strong and brave,
Who lifted the stones that lay on the ground
That became the walls of Jerusalem.

Noah's story

The verses below could be said with mime to retell the story of Noah.

Noah built a house to float,
Noah built a wooden boat,
Took inside his wife and sons,
Animals and food for everyone.
God shut the door upon them all.
They waited for the rain to fall.

Chorus:
Eight people in the boat
  Hold up eight fingers.
And it rained all day.
  Mime rainfall.
They tossed on the stormy sea –
  Rock from side to side.
Eight people in the boat
  Hold up eight fingers.
Who'd heard God say,
  Cup ear.
'You're safe if you trust in me.'
  Hold out hands, palms up.

The days went by inside the ark,
Animals and people in the dark.
They felt the waters toss about.
They wondered when they would get out.
They trusted God it was safe inside.
They could wait till the storms had died.

At last, a day with no more rain.
The water's going down again.
The tossing and the rocking stop.
The boat is on a mountain top.
Open the window to see outside
And wait until the ground has dried!

No more need for a house to float!
No more need for a wooden boat!
Now the earth is safe and dry.
See the rainbow in the sky!
Open the door and feel the sun!
Give praise to God for what he's done!

6. 6. 6. 6.

Abraham and Sarah

Traditional tune

Ab - ra - ham and Sa - rah,   Ab - ra - ham and Sa - rah,

Ab - ra - ham and Sa - rah,   Set off for a new land.

This song can be used as a game following the instructions in italics.

Two children are chosen as Abraham and Sarah. During the first verse, they walk along, arm in arm, everyone else following and singing.

Abraham and Sarah, *Sing three times*
Set off for a new land.

Everyone stands still.
God promised to be with them, *Sing three times*
And they believed in him.

Walk again as for verse 1.
They travelled and they travelled, *Sing three times*
To get to the new land.

Stand still, looking around.
At last they came to Canaan, *Sing three times*
The land God chose for them.

Everyone sits down.
They knew that God was with them, *Sing three times*
And still believed in him.

Hush-a-bye Moses

Hush-a-bye Moses, what shall we do
Rock arms.
If the soldiers should come and get you?
Hold up hands in horror.
Make a small basket
'Plait' fingers together.
Covered with tar.
Mime brushing.
Nobody'll know or guess where you are!
Smile and shake head.

Hush-a-bye Moses, cosy and warm.
Rock arms.
Miriam watches to keep you from harm.
Shade eyes.
Down by the river
Ripple fingers.
What does she see?
Shade eyes.
The basket is floating, as safe as can be.
Cup hands together and 'float' along.

Hush-a-bye Moses, who's coming here?
Rock 'baby'.
The king's daughter finds you, there's no need to fear.
Smile and shake head.
She'll see you're looked after –
Rock arms.
Miriam runs,
Run on spot.
Brings back your mother to nurse you again.
Rock arms.

Esau and Jacob

Here is Esau and his twin,
Hold up thumbs, side by side.
Jacob is his name.
But these brothers aren't good friends.
Move thumbs aside.
Isn't that a shame?
Shake head.

One day, Jacob tricked his brother.
Wriggle right thumb.
Esau, he was mad!
Shake left thumb.
Jacob ran away from home,
Move right thumb behind back.
Feeling scared and sad.

Home again came brother Jacob,
Move right thumb back slowly.
After years away.
But he wondered, 'What will Esau
Think or do or say?'

Esau ran to meet his brother,
Move left thumb towards right.
Jacob bowed down low.
Move right thumb up and down.
Jacob said, 'I'm sorry, Esau!'
Esau said, 'Hello!'

Esau forgave Jacob,
Hold up thumbs, side by side.
So the trouble ends,
Now the family is happy,
Because the twins are friends.

The spies' chant

Twelve men went to spy on Canaan.
Ten were bad and two were good.
What did they see when they spied on Canaan?
Ten were bad and two were good.
Some saw giants big and tall,
Some saw grapes in clusters fall,
Two saw God was in it all.
Ten were bad and two were good.

Here are Abraham and Sarah

Here are Ab - ra - ham and Sa - rah, Here are
Ab - ra - ham and Sa - rah, Here are Ab - ra - ham and
Sa - rah, Just a lit - tle fa - mi - ly.

Two children are chosen to be Abraham and Sarah. Everyone else forms a ring and walks round, singing.

Here are Abraham and Sarah,
Sing three times
Just a little family.

Then God sent them baby Isaac,
Sing three times
And he joined the family.
Abraham and Sarah choose another child to be Isaac and join them in the centre of the ring.

Isaac found a wife, Rebecca,
Sing three times
And she joined the family.
Isaac chooses someone to be Rebecca and go into the centre.

They had twins, Jacob and Esau,
Sing three times
And they joined the family.
Rebecca chooses two sons.

Then those boys had lots of children,
Sing three times
And they joined the family.
Everyone already in the ring chooses another to join in.

Many, many other people,
Sing three times
Came to join the family.
Everyone in the centre of the ring chooses until everybody is together in a group.

And so God had kept his promise,
Sing three times
Made a big, big family.

King David danced

Use this rhyme after telling the story of David bringing the Covenant Box back to Jerusalem. It links David's worship with our own.

King David danced,
King David sang,
He danced and sang along the way.
King David praised
And thanked the Lord,
Just as we have done (or will do) today!

Joseph was alone

Traditional tune

Jo - seph was a - lone, Jo - seph was a - lone,

Down in E - gypt, Jo - seph was a - lone.

*Hold hands in a ring
and walk in a circle.*
Joseph was alone,
Joseph was alone,
Down in Egypt,
Joseph was alone.

Stand still, clapping.
God took care of him,
God took care of him,
Down in Egypt,
God took care of him.

Move round in the ring again.
His family were at home,
His family were at home,
Still in Canaan,
His family were at home.

Stand still, clapping.
God took care of them,
God took care of them,
Back in Canaan,
God took care of them.

*Hold hands, move into
centre of ring and out again.*
Together once again,
Together once again.
All in Egypt,
Together once again.

When God gave the laws to Moses

Here is the mountain, rocky and high,
Make mountain shape with hands.

Here is the thick cloud in the sky,
Cloud shapes with thumb/forefinger.

Here are the people waiting by,
Use fingers as people.

When God gave the laws to Moses.
Palms together like two stone tablets.

Here is the lightning seen from the ground,
Draw zig-zag shapes in the air.

Here is the roar of the thunder's sound,
Pat hands on knees very fast.

Here is the smoke that billowed around,
Wave arms about.

When God gave the laws to Moses.
Put palms together.

You and I can keep the laws, too.
Point to others and then self.

It says in the Bible just what to do.
Point forefinger.

The laws are there to help me and you.
Everyone holds hands.

Thank God for the laws he gave Moses.
Raise arms.

The long walk

Walk briskly on spot.
'Let's go for a walk,' Moses said,
'While our masters are tucked up in bed!
We'll go right away –
Not just for a day!
God says that it's time that we fled.'

Still walking, mime packing, then carrying bundle.
So the Israelites packed through the night,
All they could carry – that's right!
Together and free,
Towards the Red Sea,
They hurried before it was light.

Keep walking, then stop suddenly.
But when they arrived at the sea,
They wondered, 'Whatever can be?'
No bridge was in sight,
But surely God's right
When he said, 'I will guide. Follow me!'

Moses prayed. Then, in front of their eyes,
Was a path through the water – surprise!
The waves were piled high,
Walk briskly on spot.
So they hurried by
And remembered God never tells lies!

Keep walking, more slowly.
The walk carried on, oh so long,
With sometimes a moan, then a song!
Just as you must do
When you're walking too,
And some of your friends trail along!

Keep walking, but slower and slower, stopping on last word of verse.

But at last God told them to stop,
Their feet ached – they felt they could drop!
He'd brought them safe home
To a place all their own.
The long walk was over. They'd STOP!

God was with David

God was with David all day long,
With him to make him brave and strong.

God was there when he took his sheep,
Looking for grass on the mountains steep.

David knew God was taking care
Of each of us, all day, everywhere.

David wasn't afraid of the lion or bear.
Why should he be if God was there?

God was with him all the night,
When he slept out under the stars so bright.

Did you know God is taking care
Of each of us, all day, everywhere?

Follow the leader – Joshua

'I want somebody brave and strong
To teach my people to obey.
I will be with him his whole life long
I want him to do just as I say.'
Follow the leader, Joshua!

'March round Jericho seven times,
But no one is to say a word.'
Down came the walls with a mighty crash,
When the shout of all the people was heard.
Follow the leader, Joshua!

God said to Joshua

*Everyone says lines 1 and 3 with a leader saying line 2 to retell the
Bible story.*

God said to Joshua,
'You lead the people and
I will be with you.'

God said to Joshua,
'Go to the river and
I will be with you.'

God said to Joshua,
'Take the box into the river and
I will be with you.'

God said to Joshua,
'I will dry up the river and
I will be with you.'

God said to Joshua,
'Let the people cross over and
I will be with you.'

God said to Joshua,
'Build the stones to remember that
I will be with you – ALWAYS.'

Where is Gideon?

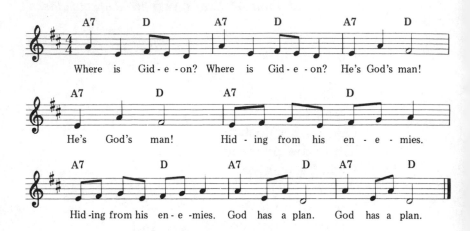

Where is Gid-e-on? Where is Gid-e-on? He's God's man!

He's God's man! Hid-ing from his en-e-mies.

Hid-ing from his en-e-mies. God has a plan. God has a plan.

Where is Gideon? Where is Gideon?
Hold hand above eyes.

He's God's man. He's God's man.
Left fist across chest on 'He's', right fist across chest on 'man'.

Hiding from his enemies. Hiding from his enemies.
Crouch: arms bent to shield face.

God has a plan. God has a plan.
Stand up straight and point upwards.

Further verses can be added by changing the third line as follows:

Verse 2: Counting all his soldiers.
Point at people nearby as though counting.

Verse 3: Blowing on his trumpet.
One hand held in front of mouth, the other waving as though flourishing a torch.

Verse 4: Chasing all his enemies.
Run on the spot.

God the helper

Music: John Baker

Gid - e - on had to help his ___ friends, He
said he couldn't go. ___ But God said, 'You can
do it. I will help ___ you!' ___

David's job was very hard,
For he was rather young.
But God said, 'You can do it.
I will help you.'

Friends of God should be like them,
Although at times it's hard.
But God says, 'You can do it.
I will help you.'

Building the Temple

This is Solomon, a wise, rich king
Hold up thumb or fist.
Who wanted to build a beautiful Temple
Mime building.
Where people could worship God.
Lift hands.

These are the men who chiselled the stone
Mime chiselling.
To build the strong walls for the beautiful Temple
Mime building.
Where people could worship God.
Lift hands.

These are the men who carried the stone
Mime carrying heavy stones.
To build strong walls for the beautiful Temple
Mime building.
Where people could worship God.
Lift hands.

These are the men who chopped the trees
Mime chopping down trees.
And sawed the wood for the beautiful Temple
Mime sawing.
Where people could worship God.
Lift hands.

These are the men who used the gold
Stroke open palm with other hand.
And carved the wood in the beautiful Temple
Mime carving.
Where people could worship God.
Lift hands.

These are the crowds who went along
Hold up fingers.
To say, 'Thank you,' for the beautiful Temple
Where people could worship God.

Ahab and Elijah

The children could mime the story.

King Ahab and Queen Jezebel,
King and queen of Israel,
Did not worship God the true,
Or do the things he told them to.

Here's King Ahab with his crown,
And a very angry frown,
Because Elijah's come to say,
'You're not doing things God's way.
God will stop the rainy rain,
'Til you turn to him again.'

This bad news makes Ahab mad,
Instead of sorry and very sad.
'How dare you threaten me?' he cried.
God told Elijah he must hide.

Elijah hid beside a stream,
Which gave him water, fresh and clean,
And God made sure he'd food to eat,
By sending ravens bringing meat.

The rain stopped falling from that day,
Because the king would not obey.
But safe and well Elijah stayed,
Because he trusted and obeyed.

Little baby Joash

Tune: 'Little Baby Moses', No 17, Come and Sing, Scripture Union.

Little baby Joash,
Hiding from the queen.
Hush, hush, hide away,
You must not be seen.

The baby's aunty took him,
Hid him well away.
Hush, hush, hide away,
You'll be king one day.

Standing in the Temple,
Joash, crowned as king.
Father God still cares for you,
Hear the people sing!

Little baby Joash,
God took care of you.
And, if we will trust him,
He'll care for us, too.

Ezra

Here are the people,
Hold up fingers and thumbs, very still.
Crowds of Israelites,
Standing still and listening
With all their might.

Here stands Ezra,
Hold up one thumb.
Up above them all,
Reading all the words of God,
From a great scroll.

Here are all the people,
Hold up fingers and thumbs, all bent.
Crowds of Israelites,
Very sad and crying
With all their might.

Here are Ezra and his friends,
Hold up one thumb and two fingers.
Telling everyone,
'God wants us all to be his friends!
Don't be so glum!'

Here are all the people,
Hold up fingers and thumbs, dancing them about.
Crowds of Israelites,
Singing, dancing, laughing
With all their might.

Here are all the people,
Hold up fingers and thumbs and smile.
Crowds of Israelites,
Happy now and thanking God
With all their might.

Jonah

God said, 'Jonah! Jonah!
I know what's best for you.
I want to teach you to do what I say
And make me glad.'

But Jonah didn't want to listen.
He ran and ran and ran away.
Then he climbed up, up, up, into a great, big ship.
It sailed far, far away.

God said, 'Jonah! Jonah!
I care about those bad people,
And I want to teach you to do what I say
And make me glad.'

But Jonah didn't want to listen.
He climbed down, down, down into the bottom of the ship.
Then he curled up and fell fast asleep.
Whoooooooooooooooooooooooo!
The storm winds blew and the boat rocked to and fro.

God said, 'Jonah! Jonah!
I care about those bad people,
And I want to teach you to do what I say
And make me glad.'

But Jonah didn't want to listen.
He was tossed into the sea.
Down, down, down he went into the big, big fish.
'Help me, God!' shouted Jonah.
Whoosh! Out of the fish Jonah popped
On to the safe, safe beach.

God said, 'Jonah! Jonah!
I care about those bad people,
And I want to teach you to do what I say
And make me glad.'

And this time Jonah listened.
And he got up and went off
To do what God had told him to.

Sing a song of Christmas

Traditional tune

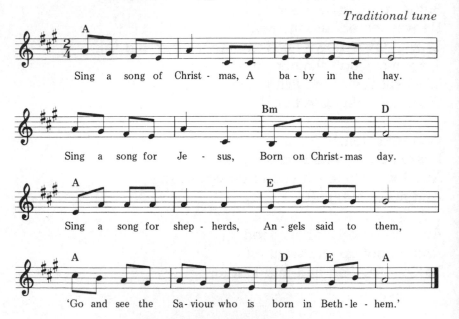

Sing a song of Christ - mas, A ba - by in the hay.

Sing a song for Je - sus, Born on Christ - mas day.

Sing a song for shep - herds, An - gels said to them,

'Go and see the Sa - viour who is born in Beth - le - hem.'

Sing a song of Christmas,
A baby in the hay.
Sing a song for Jesus,
Born on Christmas Day.
Sing a song of shepherds,
Angels said to them,
'Go and see the Saviour
Who is born in Bethlehem.'

Sing a song of wise men
Following a star,
Bringing gifts to Jesus,
Travelling so far.
Sing a song for Jesus,
Lying in the hay,
Born to make us happy,
Born for us on Christmas Day.

SURPRISES

Use the next four rhymes to retell the Christmas story. Children can join in the last line of each verse.

Mary's surprise

Mary knows just who she is,
Jewish girl with big, dark eyes,
But she doesn't know she'll have
A big surprise!

Mary knows she'll marry soon,
Marry Joseph, kind and wise,
But she doesn't know she'll have
A big surprise!

Mary knows that God is good.
Mary knows that God is wise,
But she doesn't know she'll have
A big surprise!

Mary's sitting quietly,
Jewish girl with big, dark eyes,
When an angel tells her of
Her big surprise!

Mary is in Bethlehem,
She's a mother, kind and wise.
Now she knows that Jesus is
God's big surprise!

Joseph's surprise

One night, Joseph's very sad,
Goes to sleep and shuts his eyes.
Dreams about an angel with
A big surprise!

In the morning, Joseph's glad,
Opens wide his happy eyes.
Now he knows that Jesus is
God's big surprise!

Joseph marries Mary soon,
Jewish girl with big, dark eyes.
Cares for her and waits to see
Their big surprise!

All the way to Bethlehem,
Underneath the sunny skies,
Joseph takes good care to guard
The big surprise!

In a room in Bethlehem,
Mary hears her baby's cries.
Joseph knows that Jesus is
God's big surprise!

Shepherds' surprise

Watching sheep near Bethlehem,
Sitting under starry skies,
Suddenly, some shepherds have
A big surprise!

Angels sing a song to them,
Tell them where a baby lies.
Shepherds hurry off to see
Their big surprise!

See the shepherds hurry back!
Smiling faces, happy eyes!
Now they know that Jesus is
God's big surprise!

Wise Men's surprise

Far away and far away,
Looking at the starry skies,
Suddenly some wise men have
A big surprise!

One bright star appears and then
Seems to move across the skies.
So they start their journey to
Their big surprise!

On and on the wise men go,
Staring at the starry skies,
Till they find and kneel before
Their big surprise!

See the wise men travel home!
Smiling faces, happy eyes!
Now they know that Jesus is
God's big surprise!

Great wise men

Great wise men lived in the East.
God sent a star so bright
To call the men to Bethlehem
And guide them by its light.

Great wise men set out at once,
Prepared to travel far.
With gold and perfumes rare and old,
They followed the bright star.

Great wise men reached Bethlehem
They found a baby boy,
Lord Jesus sent to fill the world
With hope and love and joy.

Follow the light

Do appropriate actions with this rhyme.

Look up, look up, see the star
Shining on Bethlehem so far.
Ride, ride, follow the light
Through the day and through the night.
Bow, bow to the family
And Jesus on his mother's knee.
Give our gifts to the Prince of Love
Wave thank you to the star above.

Sweet Mary

Music: Joan Stride

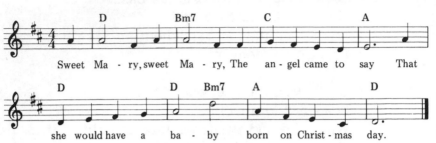

Sweet Ma - ry, sweet Ma - ry, The an - gel came to say That
she would have a ba - by born on Christ - mas day.

Sweet Mary, sweet Mary,
The angel came to say
That she would have a baby,
Born on Christmas Day.

Lord Jesus, Lord Jesus,
Sleeping on the straw,
Born in a humble stable,
But King for evermore.

The angels, the angels,
Sang praises for his birth,
'Glory to God in heaven
And peace to men on earth.'

The shepherds, the shepherds,
Heard the angels sing
And hurried with their message
To see the new born King.

The wise men, the wise men,
Were looking for the King,
Led onwards by a bright star,
They came to worship him.

Sing people, be joyful,
How happy we can be
As we think of that baby,
God's gift to you and me!

Babies

Rock the baby in my arms.
Mime rocking baby.

Hold him snug and tight.

Lay him in his little cot
Mime putting baby down.

And gently kiss goodnight.
Kiss hand.

Dear Father God, keep babies
Mime rocking baby.

In your loving care.

Thank you for sending Jesus

For us all to share.
Mime holding baby out to others.

Jesus in Jerusalem

'Where is Jesus? Where is Jesus?'
Look left and right.

Mary and Joseph say.

'Is he in the market place?
Shake head.

We can't find him today!'
Open hands in despair.

'Where is Jesus? Where is Jesus?'
Look left and right.

Mary and Joseph say.

'Is he in the busy streets?
Shake head.

We can't find him today!'
Open hands in despair.

'Where is Jesus? Where is Jesus?'
Look left and right.

Mary and Joseph say.

'He is in the Temple-church.

We have found him today!'
Clap hands.

Just like you and I do

Use the rhyme to link the growth and change children experience to that Jesus experienced.

When Jesus was a tiny baby
Rock arms.

He was so sweet and small and new.

And he grew and grew and grew
Let arm rise higher and higher.

Just like you and I do.
Point to others and self.

When Jesus was a little boy
Show height.

He liked to play and have fun too,
Clap hands.

And he grew and grew and grew
Let arm rise higher and higher.

Just like you and I do.
Point to others and self.

When Jesus was a bigger boy
Show height.

He helped his sisters, brothers too,

And he grew and grew and grew
Let arm rise higher and higher.

Just like you and I do.
Point to others and self.

It's fun waking up in the morning

Music: Millicent Slack

It's fun wak-ing up in the morn-ing And watch-ing the dark-ness go, ___ Just as Je-sus did in Na-za-reth long a-go.

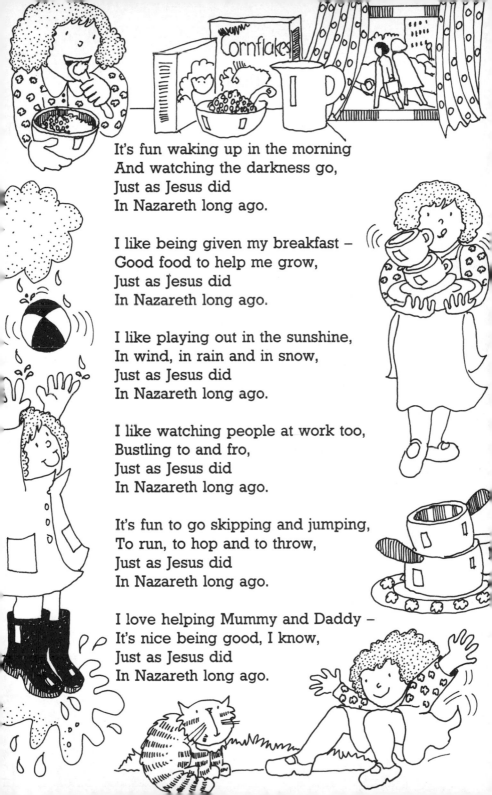

It's fun waking up in the morning
And watching the darkness go,
Just as Jesus did
In Nazareth long ago.

I like being given my breakfast –
Good food to help me grow,
Just as Jesus did
In Nazareth long ago.

I like playing out in the sunshine,
In wind, in rain and in snow,
Just as Jesus did
In Nazareth long ago.

I like watching people at work too,
Bustling to and fro,
Just as Jesus did
In Nazareth long ago.

It's fun to go skipping and jumping,
To run, to hop and to throw,
Just as Jesus did
In Nazareth long ago.

I love helping Mummy and Daddy –
It's nice being good, I know,
Just as Jesus did
In Nazareth long ago.

Jesus is!

(This rhyme should be spoken rhythmically and with enthusiasm!)

Jesus is, Jesus is, Jesus is
WONDERFUL! (*Clap three times.*)
Jesus is, Jesus is, Jesus is,
OUR FRIEND! (*Raise hands.*)

He loves us.
He helps us
To know what's right and wrong.

He's kind.
He cares.
He's with us all day long.

Jesus is, Jesus is, Jesus is
WONDERFUL! (*Clap three times.*)
Jesus is, Jesus is, Jesus is
OUR FRIEND! (*Raise hands.*)

Do you know who Jesus is?

Do you know who Jesus is?
Is he the Son of God?
He turned some water into wine.
Yes, he's the Son of God.

Do you know who Jesus is?
Is he the Son of God?
He calmed the stormy wind and waves.
Yes, he's the Son of God.

Do you know who Jesus is?
Is he the Son of God?
He healed the blind and deaf and lame.
Yes, he's the Son of God.

Do you know who Jesus is?
Is he the Son of God?
He died but came alive again.
Yes, he's the Son of God.

Do you know who Jesus is?
Is he the Son of God?
He lives today and he's our friend.
Yes, he's the Son of God.

He's the Son of God

Je - sus died then came a - live, Je - sus died then came a -
live, Je - sus died then came a - live He's the Son of God.

Jesus died then came alive,
Jesus died then came alive,
Jesus died then came alive,
He's the Son of God.

Jesus made ill people better,
He's the Son of God.

Jesus always answers prayers,
He's the Son of God.

We must try to learn about him,
He's the Son of God.

We can all be friends of Jesus,
He's the Son of God.

He has promised to be with us,
He's the Son of God.

He will help us to be like him,
He's the Son of God.

*This song and the previous rhyme aim to show some of the special
qualities and actions of Jesus which lie behind the title 'Son of God'.*

Jesus is my friend!

Music: John Baker

Je-sus is my friend, Je-sus is my friend. The fish-er-men knew that they could say, 'Yes, Je-sus is my friend.'

Jesus is my friend,
Jesus is my friend.
Rich or poor, we all can say,
'Yes, Jesus is my friend!'

Jesus is my friend,
Jesus is my friend.
Brothers, sisters, all can say,
'Yes, Jesus is my friend!'

Jesus is my friend,
Jesus is my friend.
Wherever I go, I can say,
'Yes, Jesus is my friend!'

Andrew, Andrew

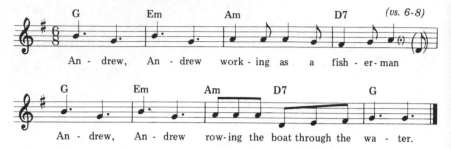

An - drew, An - drew work - ing as a fish - er- man

An - drew, An - drew row-ing the boat through the wa - ter.

Andrew, Andrew, working as a fisherman.
Andrew, Andrew, rowing the boat through the water.
Mime rowing boat throughout verse.

Andrew, Andrew, working as a fisherman.
Andrew, Andrew, dropping the nets in the water.
Mime picking up and throwing out nets.

Andrew, Andrew, working as a fisherman.
Andrew, Andrew, pulling the nets full of fishes.
Mime hauling in nets.

Andrew, Andrew, working as a fisherman.
Andrew, Andrew, bringing the fish to the people.
Mime carrying large basket.

Andrew, Andrew, working as a friend of Jesus.
Andrew, Andrew, living and sharing with him.
Mime sharing out food.

Andrew, Andrew, working as a friend of Jesus.
Andrew, Andrew, listening and learning from him.
Cup hand behind ear.

Andrew, Andrew, working as a friend of Jesus.
Andrew, Andrew, helping friend Jesus each day.
Hold hands with neighbour, swing arms.

Jairus' daughter

Here is the daughter feeling very ill.
Point to little finger.

Here is the doctor. He cannot make her well.
Point to thumb.

Here is the mother. She's feeling most upset.
Point to index finger.

Here is the father. He hurries to get Jesus.
Point to third finger.

Point to middle finger.
Jesus will help them. He's kind, brave and strong.
Jesus will help them. He's hurrying along
To the house by the lake where the little girl lies.
He'll soon make her better. It's such a surprise –
For her mother (*index finger*) and father (*third finger*)
and everyone there (*all fingers*).
Jesus has shown them his power and his care.

A blind man

Music: Joan Stride

A   man called Je - sus took some mud and put it   on my eyes.
He told   me   I should go and wash and then to my sur -prise,

How won - der - ful, how won - der - ful, I found that I could see!
How won - der - ful, how won - der - ful, what Je - sus did for me!

A man called Jesus took some mud
And put it on my eyes.
He told me I should go and wash
And then to my surprise,
How wonderful, how wonderful,
I found that I could see!
How wonderful, how wonderful,
What Jesus did for me!

Slowly, slowly, poor old lady

Slowly, slowly, poor old lady,
Walk slowly on the spot with back bent.

With her bent back sore and aching,

Goes to church where she meets Jesus.
Look up and straighten slowly.

What a happy day he's making!

Gladly, gladly, straight old lady,
Walk quickly on the spot, smiling.

With a strong back, quickly walking

Home from church where Jesus helped her.

She is smiling, laughing, talking!

Martha and Mary

Here is busy Martha,
Hold up left thumb or a puppet.

Working all the day.
Move it about.

Too busy to listen to Jesus,

Too busy to hear what he'd say.

Here is listening Mary,
Hold up right thumb or another puppet.

Listening all the day.
Keep it still.

Wanting to listen to Jesus,

Wanting to hear what he'd say.

People Jesus helped

Music: Elizabeth Hume

Here is a sad man, a sad man, a sad man.

Here is a sad man, but Je - sus made him glad. ____

This song can be used as a ring game with one child at the centre pretending to be a person whom Jesus helped. Everyone else, walking around in a ring, sings the song. Another child is chosen to be the central character for each new verse.

Here is a sad man, a sad man, a sad man.
Here is a sad man, but Jesus made him glad.

Everyone stands and claps while the child in the centre walks around smiling.

Now he is happy, is happy, is happy.
Now he is happy. Jesus made him glad.

Here is a lame man, a lame man, a lame man.
Here is a lame man, but Jesus made him well.

Everyone stands and claps while the child in the centre runs and jumps.

He can run and jump now, jump now, jump now.
He can run and jump now. Jesus made him well.

Here is a blind man, a blind man, a blind man.
Here is a blind man. Jesus made him well.

Everyone stands and claps while the child in the centre mimes seeing again.

He can look and see now, see now, see now.
He can look and see now. Jesus made him well.

Here is a deaf man, a deaf man, a deaf man.
Here is a deaf man. Jesus made him well.

Everyone stands and claps while the child in the centre walks around the circle with hand behind ear, listening to the singing.

He can hear and listen, listen, listen.
He can hear and listen. Jesus made him well.

Enough for all!

Use this rhyme to tell or retell the Bible story to children.

There was a boy out for the day,
All he had for lunch,
Were two tiny silver fish –
Bread with it to munch!

He wrapped it up so very tight,
Carefully he planned,
To eat it all at dinner time,
Sitting on the sand!

But while he was out walking,
Along by the seashore
Listening to Jesus' words,
A big crowd he saw.

The boy just stood there watching,
The crowd grew bigger still,
Some had to come to listen, but
Some were very ill!

Jesus kindly talked to them,
Healed those who were weak,
So they stayed all day, but had
Nothing much to eat.

When Jesus saw their hungry looks,
He said, 'They must be fed.
Is there someone in this crowd
Who's brought any bread?'

The boy replied, 'Yes, sir, I have
A lunch of bread and fish.
I'll share it with you willingly
If that is what you wish.'

So Jesus took the bread and fish,
Gave thanks and broke it neat.
And everyone, five thousand there,
Had enough to eat!

And when they came to sweep the crumbs,
As everyone should do,
Twelve basketfuls were gathered in.
Such a small lunch too!

Jesus feeds the crowd

Music: Joan Stride

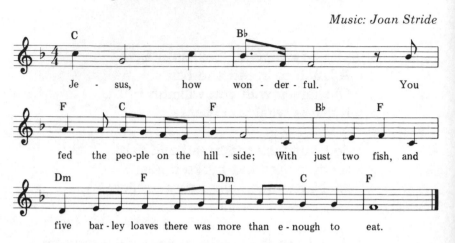

Je - sus, how won - der - ful. You fed the peo-ple on the hill - side; With just two fish, and five bar - ley loaves there was more than e - nough to eat.

Jesus, how wonderful!
You fed the people on the hillside;
With just two fish and five barley loaves
There was more than enough to eat!

Two fish and five little loaves

This is the boy
Hold up index finger.

Who had two fish,
Hold up two fingers on other hand.

One, two fish,

And five little loaves.
Hold up five fingers.

One, two, three four, five little loaves.

He gave them to Jesus.
Hold out hands.

Here are the people,
Hold up ten fingers.

Listening to Jesus.
Hands behind ears.

They had no food.
Rub tummy.

Jesus thanked God for
Hold up hands.

The five little loaves *five fingers.*

And two little fish. *two fingers.*

Then shared them with all the people.
Mime sharing.

One hundred sheep

One hundred sheep I had with me,
Spread arms wide then point to self.
But one has gone astray.
Point into distance.
Where, oh where can that sheep be?
Shrug shoulders.
I must find her today.
Shield eyes.

Everywhere I seemed to look,
Look all around.
By river, hill and tree.
Ripple fingers, make arch for hill, spread arms above head.
Then I saw her by the brook;
Point and smile.
Happy, happy me!
Point to self.

Sheep and shepherd

This rhyme provides background material for any Bible story about shepherds.

One flock of woolly sheep settling down to lunch,
Green grass,
Very good,
Munch, munch, munch.

Joseph the shepherd settling down to lunch,
Bread and cheese,
Very good,
Munch, munch, munch.

A son took his money

This rhyme could be used to retell the Bible story, possibly with mime.

A son took his money
And went far away
To buy all the things
That he wanted, one day.

His father was sad
That his dear son was gone,
While the son spent his money,
And had lots of fun!

Soon his money was gone,
No food could be had.
He looked after pigs
And was hungry and sad.

He went home to his father
And said, 'I am sorry.'
His father forgave him,
And gave a big party!

The two builders

A wise man wanted to build a house.
Make flat-topped house with hands.
He found some land that was firm.
Shade eyes.
He dug deep through the rocky soil
Mime digging.
And began to build the walls.
Place hand on hand, hand on hand.
He worked and worked until, at last,
His house was quite complete.
Form house as before.
But then one night, as he lay in bed,
The wind began to blow.
Make noise of wind.

The sky grew dark,
Cover eyes with hands.
Lightning flashed,
Take hands away quickly.
Rain came pouring down.
Mime rain falling with fingers.
The strong wind howled,
Make noise of wind.
Thunder crashed,
Stamp.
Floods came rising up.
With palms up, lift hands.

The wise man knew his house was safe
Because it was built on the rock.
Form house as before.

A foolish man went to build a house.
Repeat actions as before.
He found some land that was soft.
He dug quickly through the sandy soil
And began to build the walls.
The work was easy, and very soon
His house was quite complete.
But then one night, as he lay in bed,
The wind began to blow.

The sky grew dark,
Lightning flashed,
Rain came pouring down.
The strong wind howled,
Thunder crashed,
Floods came rising up.

But this man's house came tumbling down
Form house, then drop hands into lap.
Because it was built on sand.

The lost coin

'Wherever can it be?' said the lady
When she lost a silver coin.
'I've only got nine, I should have ten.
  Hold up nine fingers, then ten.
Wherever can it be?'

'Wherever can it be?' said the lady
And she went to light her lamp.
  Hold palm up.
She swept the floor, looked under the chairs.
  Mime sweeping.
'Wherever can it be?'

'Wherever can it be?' said the lady
As she looked behind the doors.
  Mime opening door.
She searched the room, looked under the beds.
  Mime searching.
'Wherever can it be?'

'There it is!' said the lady happily
When she found her silver coin.
  Make circle with thumb and forefinger.
She jumped for joy, she was so glad, so she
  Jump and smile at each other.
Asked all her friends to tea.

The mustard seed

A man took a mustard seed,
Mime picking tiny seed from palm.
A very tiny mustard seed,
And planted it in the ground.
Mime planting seed.

The rain rained,
Mime rain falling.
The sun shone,
Open hands and raise arms.
And some leaves began to grow.
Palms together, open fingers out slowly.
And soon the mustard seed,
Mime picking seed from palm.
The very tiny mustard seed,
Became a very big plant.
Arms together, hands out at face height.

The rain rained,
Mime rain falling.
The sun shone
Open hands and raise arms.
And the branches began to grow.
Arms together, hands out and moving apart.

And soon the mustard seed,
Mime picking seed from palm.
The very tiny mustard seed
Had become a mustard tree!
Arms raised and widely apart.

The road from Jerusalem to Jericho

This is the story,
That Jesus once told,
About a rich man
  Walk on spot, looking around.
Walking down the road,
From Jerusalem to Jericho.

Out jumped some robbers,
So cruel and bad,
And mugged the rich man
  Mime punching and grabbing purse.
Walking down the road
  Repeat walking on the spot as before.
From Jerusalem to Jericho.

Along came a priest.
He walked quickly past
Walk quickly on spot, looking ahead.
That man lying hurt,
Head on hands.
Mugged by robbers,
Mime as before.
Cruel and bad, as
He walked down the road
Mime as before
From Jerusalem to Jericho.

Next came a Levite.
Walk on the spot.
He looked . . . then walked by
Stop, look and walk on.
The man lying hurt,
Repeat actions as before.
Mugged by robbers,
Cruel and bad, as
He walked down the road
From Jerusalem to Jericho.

The Samaritan . . .
Walk on spot.
Stopped. Then he cared for
Stop, stoop and mime lifting.
The man lying hurt,
Repeat actions as before.
Mugged by robbers,
Cruel and bad, as
He walked down the road
From Jerusalem to Jericho.

He's off to Jerusalem

Sing a song and shout for joy,
Happy is each girl and boy.
Shout for King Jesus!
He's off to Jerusalem.

Chorus:
He's off to Jerusalem,
He's off to Jerusalem,
Riding on a donkey.
He's off to Jerusalem.

It was early in the day.
Jesus started on his way.
Wave all your branches!
He's off to Jerusalem.

Shout 'Hosanna!' everyone,
For we know he is God's Son.
Shout for King Jesus.
He's off to Jerusalem.

Praise God! Hallelujah!

Music: Joan Stride

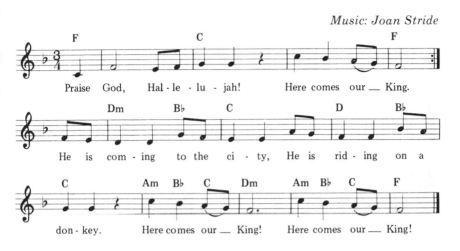

A processional song for Palm Sunday, which can be used with waving branches, music and percussion.

Praise God! Hallelujah!
Here comes our King.
Praise God! Hallelujah!
Here comes our King.
He is coming to the city,
He is riding on a donkey.
Here comes our King!
Here comes our King!

Jesus said, 'Let's go into town'

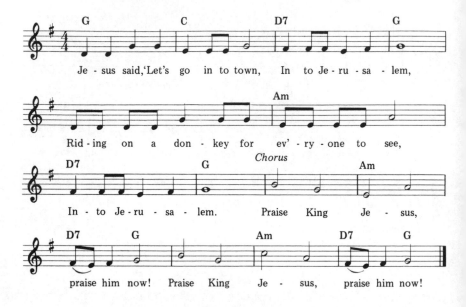

Je - sus said, 'Let's go in to town, In to Je - ru - sa - lem,

Rid - ing on a don - key for ev' - ry - one to see,

In - to Je - ru - sa - lem. Praise King Je - sus,

praise him now! Praise King Je - sus, praise him now!

Jesus said, 'Let's go into town,
Into Jerusalem,
Riding on a donkey for everyone to see,
Into Jerusalem.'

Chorus:
Praise King Jesus!
Wave arms or branches during chorus.
Praise him now!
Praise King Jesus!
Praise him now!

Jesus said, 'Let's sit down to eat,
Now in Jerusalem.
Share this loaf of bread and drink this cup of wine.
Now in Jerusalem.'

Jesus said, 'It's time for me to die,
Now in Jerusalem.
Don't be afraid, friends, I'll see you all again,
Soon in Jerusalem.'

Jesus said, 'I'm alive, can't you see,
Now and for evermore?
I'm with you for ever, I'll always be your friend,
Now and for evermore.'

Preparing the Last Supper

They used their ears to listen.
Touch ears.

They used their eyes to look.
Point to eyes.

They used their feet to follow
Point to feet.

The man with the water-pot.
Hold 'pot' on shoulder.

They used their lips to ask

For the room where they could meet.
Touch lips.

And they used their hands to cook
Show hands.

The food that they would eat.

I'm alive!

*Traditional tune
arr. John Baker*

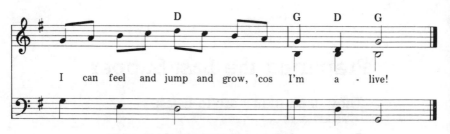

I'm alive! I'm alive!
I can feel and jump and grow
'Cos I'm alive!

He's alive! He's alive!
Jesus died and rose again.
Now he's alive!

He's alive! He's alive!
Jesus shared the bread and fish.
Now he's alive!

He's alive! He's alive!
Jesus said, 'I'll be with you.'
'Cos he's alive!

We have seen the Lord

Music: Joan Stride

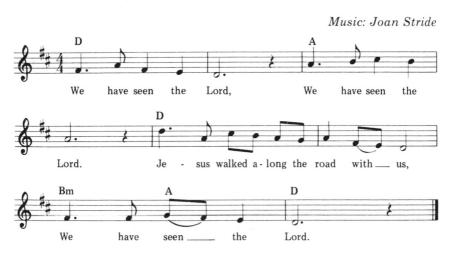

The song should be used with drama, children acting the parts of the characters in the stories. These can be found in Luke 24:13–35 and John 21:1–14.

On the road to Emmaus:
We have seen the Lord.
We have seen the Lord.
Jesus walked along the road with us.
We have seen the Lord.

By the seashore:
We have seen the Lord.
We have seen the Lord.
Jesus showed his love and care for us.
We have seen the Lord.

4, 4. 4.2 . 4.4, 4.2

8. 6 - 8. 6.

How do I know?

Music: John Baker

How do I know that this lit - tle seed is a -

live, a - live, a - live - o? With wa - ter and the sun it will

grow, grow, grow And show that it's a - live.

How do I know that this little seed
Is alive, alive, alive-o?
With water and the sun it will grow, grow, grow
And show that it's alive.

How do I know that this little creature
Is alive, alive, alive-o?
He will eat and play and will grow, grow, grow
And show that he's alive.

How do I know that all of me
Is alive, alive, alive-o?
I can run and jump and I'll grow, grow, grow
And show that I'm alive.

How do I know, even though he died
That Jesus came alive-o?
He met his friends so they all would know.
He showed he was alive.

How do I know that Jesus is my friend
And he is still alive-o?
He promised to us all it would be just so.
I know he is alive.

In the garden

In the garden was a dark, dark cave.
In the front of the cave was a big, big stone.
By the stone were strong, strong soldiers.
Inside the cave was Jesus!

Earthquake! Earth shake!
Noise and light!
Earthquake! Earth shake!
Angel bright!

In the garden was a dark, dark cave.
Beside the cave was a big, big stone.
Strong, strong soldiers had run away.
And inside the cave was – NO ONE!

Jesus was alive again!

'Remember me'

Music: Elizabeth Hume

Je - sus said, 'Re-mem - ber me!' Je - sus said, 'Re-mem-ber me!'

Je - sus said, 'Re - mem-ber me! Re - mem-ber that I love you!'——

Jesus said, 'Remember me.'
Jesus said, 'Remember me.'
Jesus said, 'Remember me.
Remember that I love you.'

On the Day of Pentecost

Friends of Jesus met together
In a room where they could pray.
They said, 'Jesus, how we love you,
Though we can't see you today!'

Friends of Jesus, quietly waiting,
Heard a noise like rushing air,
Saw what looked like flames of fire
Rest on everybody there.

Friends of Jesus, all together,
Thanked God for his power and love.
Went outside where crowds of people
Heard them praising God above!

Friends of Jesus – up spoke Peter,
Told the crowd, 'You ought to know -
God sent you his own Son, Jesus.
Be his friends too. Don't be slow!'

Friends of Jesus, many people
Joined God's family that day.
Learnt just how much Jesus loved them,
Learnt to trust him and obey.

Friends of Jesus, there are millions
Who have joined God's family.
Let's be glad that our friend, Jesus
Loves them all, including me!

Lydia

Here are Lydia and her friends.
Hold one hand upright and wriggle fingers.
Here is the flowing river.
Lay other hand flat and ripple fingers.
They love to sit upon its banks,
Actions as before.
And pray and talk together.

Here comes Paul with his three friends,
Move four fingers along.
Down to the flowing river.
Ripple fingers of other hand as before.
They join the women on the banks,
Hold hands with palms facing and wriggle fingers.
And sit and talk together.

Paul talks of his friend, Jesus.
Hold up forefinger.
Lydia listens well.
Cup ears with hands.
Then she says, 'I'd like Jesus
To be my friend as well.'
Point to self.

Lydia is happy,
Smile.
Jesus is her friend.
Cross hands over chest.
'Come and stay with me,' she says
Beckon with forefinger.
To Paul and his three friends.
Hold up four fingers and then cover them with the other hand.

Here is Paul

Here is Paul, an angry man,
Hold up one finger and 'march' it along.

Marching along the dusty road,

Going to put all the Christians in jail.

Here is Paul, a sorry man,
Curl the finger.

Kneeling down on the dusty road,

Meeting with Jesus, the Christians' friend.

Here is Paul, a thoughtful man,

Walking along the dusty road,
Move the finger along, much more slowly.

Going to tell all the Christians he's changed.

Here is Paul, a loving man,
Hold finger up straight.

Helping and caring, wherever he can,

Talking of Jesus, the Christians' friend.

Apollos

Here is Apollos,
Hold up index finger.

A very clever man.
Tap forehead.

Can he read and write well?

Yes, he can.
Nod head.

But he's not too proud to learn more!

Here is Apollos,
Hold up index finger.

Preaching to a crowd,
Hold up and wave fingers of other hand.

Talking about Jesus

Right out loud!

But he's not too proud to learn more!

Here is Apollos,
Hold up index finger.

Not talking at all.
Put hand over mouth.

Listening gladly

To some friends of Paul

Because he's not too proud to learn more!

All sorts of people

Music: Joan Stride

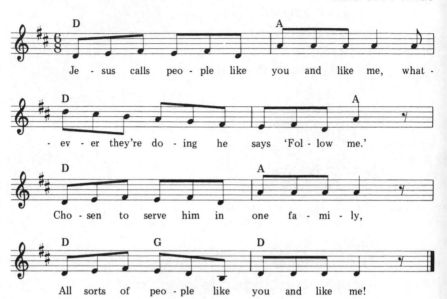

Jesus calls people like you and me.
Whatever they're doing, he says, 'Follow me.'
Chosen to serve him in one family,
All sorts of people like you and me!

Friends

The first two and last two lines of each verse can be said by everyone, a leader saying the middle lines while others mime an appropriate situation.

Friends give to their friends
Whatever they may need.
If someone is sick or sad,
This is what a friend will do,
He will give him love and care,
He will give him comfort too.
Friends give to their friends
Anything they need.

Friends give to their friends
Whatever they may need.
If someone is hungry, then,
This is what a friend will do,
He will give him food to eat,
And he'll give it gladly too.
Friends give to their friends
Anything they need.

Friends give to their friends
Whatever they may need.
If someone is poor and cold,
This is what a friend will do,
He will give him clothes to wear,
Share with him good things, too.
Friends give to their friends
Anything they need.

Belonging to the Jesus family

This can be sung with a leader singing the first lines and everyone else repeating.

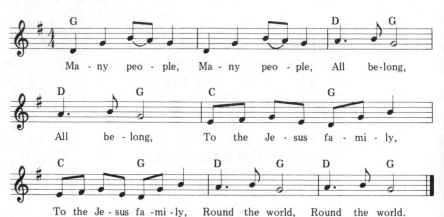

Ma - ny peo - ple, Ma - ny peo - ple, All be-long,

All be - long, To the Je - sus fa - mi - ly,

To the Je - sus fa -mi -ly, Round the world, Round the world.

Many people,
Many people,
All belong,
All belong,
To the Jesus family,
To the Jesus family,
Round the world,
Round the world.

All of us,
All of us,
Can belong,
Can belong,
To the Jesus family,
To the Jesus family,
Round the world,
Round the world.

Thank you, Jesus,
Thank you, Jesus,
We belong,
We belong,
To the Jesus family,
To the Jesus family,
Here and now,
Here and now.

Caring hands

Mummy's hands are warm and kind.
They tuck me up in bed.
Grandad's hands are hairy
And Granny's hands are red.
Doctor Jones has cold hands
Although he cures my pain.
Daddy's hands toss me high,
Then put me down again.
All these hands are loving hands,
They all take care of me.
Thank you God, for all the hands
That hold your family.

This rhyme puts substance into words like 'care' and 'love'.

Give and share

Music: J. Parmenter

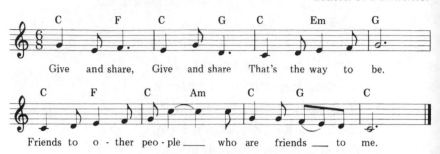

Give and share, Give and share That's the way to be.

Friends to o-ther peo-ple___ who are friends ___ to me.

Give and share, give and share,
That's the way to be
Friends to other people,
Who are friends to me.

Give and share, give and share,
That's the way to be
More like the Lord Jesus
Who gave his life for me.

We can share

We can share, We can share, When we're friends,

When we're friends If we share with o-thers,

If we share with o-thers, God is glad, God is glad.

We can share, we can share, G C F
When we're friends, when we're friends. G C A
If we share with others, if we share with others, C Bb A G F C
God is glad, God is glad. G C F

We can play, we can play,
When we're friends.
If we play together, if we play together,
God is glad, God is glad.

We can help, we can help,
When we're friends, when we're friends.
If we help each other, if we help each other,
God is glad, God is glad.

We can give, we can give,
When we're friends, when we're friends.
If we give to others, if we give to others,
God is glad, God is glad.

We can pray, we can pray,
When we're friends, when we're friends.
If we pray for others, if we pray for others,
God is glad, God is glad.

row, row, row your boat

Wave your hands

Traditional tune

Wave, wave, wave your hands, Wave your hands and smile.
Show the world you're joy - ful, Joy - ful all the while.

Wave, wave, wave your hands,
Wave your hands and smile.
Show the world you're joyful,
Joyful all the while.

Sing, sing, sing a song,
Sing of all your joys.
Tell the world you're happy,
Happy girls and boys.

Send, send, send your love
Out across the sea.
Show the world you're caring
For all God's family.

Needing help

When I was running down the path,
I fell and hurt my knee.
I looked for someone kind to help,
But no one came to me.

My knee was cut and bleeding
And I began to cry.
Then Mummy came and helped me up,
And soon my tears were dry.

She washed my knee and found some cream
And put a plaster on.
Because she hugged me better,
Ev'ry bit of hurt is gone!

Young children need concrete examples to understand abstract words like 'help'. This rhyme reminds them of an experience of needing help and a kind, loving response.

Love your neighbour

Music: Rose Williams

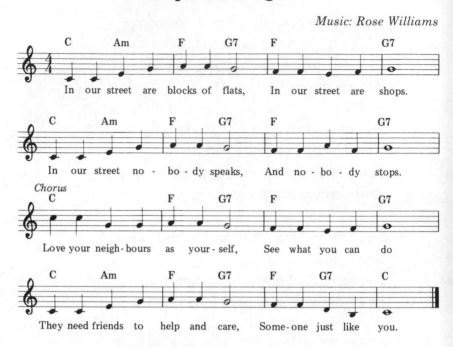

In our street are blocks of flats.
In our street are shops.
In our street nobody speaks
And nobody stops.

Chorus:

Love your neighbours as yourself,
See what you can do.
They need friends to help and care,
Someone just like you.

Stop and talk to someone old.
Stop and talk awhile.
Stop and play with someone small.
Give someone a smile.

Give someone a happy day.
You'll be happy too!
Give someone a helping hand.
Next day, they'll help you!

Friends of God

This rhyme shows that friendship with God involves all the best things about friendships with others.

Friends talk
Every day.
Friends listen
To what you say.

Friends of God
Talk to him,
And he listens
Every day.

Friends of God
Believe he hears
And will answer
All their prayers.

If friends say
They'll help you,
You can know
That's what they'll do.

Friends of God
Believe him too.
What he says
They know he'll do.

Jesus, you're always with us

Music: Joan Stride

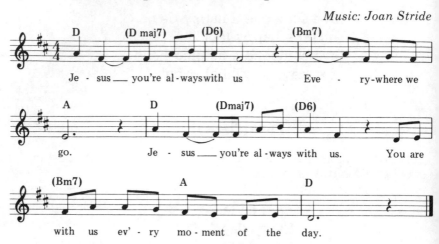

Je - sus — you're al - ways with us   Eve - ry - where we go.   Je - sus — you're al - ways with us.   You are with us ev' - ry mo - ment of the day.

Guitar chords in brackets are optional

Jesus, you're always with us,
Everywhere we go.
Jesus, you're always with us.
You are with us every moment of the day.

Busy days with Jesus

On Mondays, when I go to school,
Jesus is with me.
On Tuesdays, at the swimming pool,
Jesus is with me.
On Wednesdays, when we go to Gran's,
On Thursdays, Cubs and Brownies,
On Fridays, when I watch TV,
I'm glad he's still with me.
On Saturdays, no school today,
Jesus is with me.
On Sundays, that's a special day,
Yes, Jesus is with me!

This rhyme can be used and adapted by school-age children to affirm the presence of Jesus who is with them at all times.

Jesus is your friend

Music: Cliff Ince

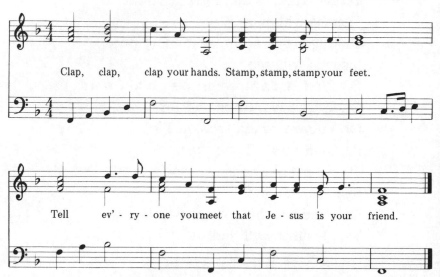

Clap, clap, clap your hands. Stamp, stamp, stamp your feet.

Tell ev' - ry - one you meet that Je - sus is your friend.

Clap, clap, clap your hands,
Stamp, stamp, stamp your feet,
Tell everyone you meet
That Jesus is your friend.

Loving Father

Music: Joan Stride

Loving Father, hear our song.
Please forgive us when we do wrong.
We have nothing to give to you
And yet you love us our whole life through.

Make God happy

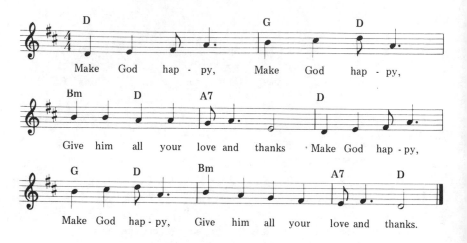

Make God happy, make God happy.
Give him all your love and thanks.
Make God happy, make God happy.
Give him all your love and thanks.

Make God happy, make God happy.
Give to others what you can.
Make God happy, make God happy.
Give to others what you can.

God is happy when we love him

Traditional tune

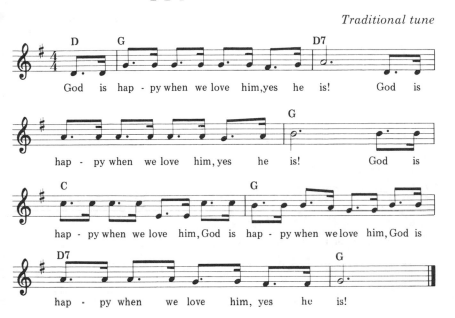

God is happy when we love him, yes he is! *Sing twice.*
God is happy when we love him, *Sing twice.*
God is happy when we love him, yes he is!

God forgives us when we're sorry, yes he does! *Sing twice.*
God forgives us when we're sorry, *Sing twice.*
God forgives us when we're sorry, yes he does!

God is happy when we're friends, yes he is! *Sing twice.*
God is happy when we're friends, *Sing twice.*
God is happy when we're friends, yes he is!

So we praise him with our voices, yes we do! *Sing twice.*
So we praise him with our voices, *Sing twice.*
So we praise him with our voices, yes we do!

Then we are friends of God

Music: *John Baker*

When you show your love, When I show my love, When
you and I both show our love, Then we are
friends of God.

When you show your love,
When I show my love,
When you and I both show our love,
Then we are friends of God.

When you talk to God,
When I talk to God,
When you and I both talk to him,
Then we are friends of God.

When you believe in God,
When I believe in God,
When you and I both believe in him,
Then we are friends of God.

When you work for God,
When I work for God,
When you and I both work for him,
Then we are friends of God.

You say, 'Thank you, God',
I say, 'Thank you, God',
When you and I say thanks to him,
Then we are friends of God.

I want to be like Jesus

This prayer can be used when hearing about how Jesus responded to people who came to him.

I want to be like Jesus,
He loved so much.
Everybody wanted
His gentle touch.
Help me, Jesus, now I pray,
To be loving, every day.

God loves and cares for me

Music: John Baker

God lis - tens when I talk to him, He hears me when I pray. God lis - tens when I talk to him, He hears me when I pray. It's ea - sy to see____ God loves and cares for me!

When I have something hard to do,
God will show me the way.
When I have something hard to do,
God will show me the way.
It's easy to see –
God loves and cares for me!

There are times when I feel afraid,
But then I know God's there.
There are times when I feel afraid,
But then I know God's there.
It's easy to see –
God loves and cares for me!

God gives me everything I need.
He shows his love for me.
God gives me everything I need.
He shows his love for me.
It's easy to see –
God loves and cares for me!

I'll try to do what God has said –
Love him and others too.
I'll try to do what God has said –
Love him and others too.
It's easy to see –
God loves and cares for me!

Get up!

Music: C. Powell and K. Wood

Chorus:

Get up out of bed,
Crouch down and jump up.

Have a yawn and scratch your head
Hand over mouth, scratch head.

And say, 'Thank you, it's a brand new day.'
*Lift right palm upwards on the word 'thank', left palm on the word
'you'.*

Stretch out, touch your toes,
Arms out, bend over.

Blink your eyes and blow your nose
Clench fists and eyes, then open, hand to nose.

And say, 'Thank you, it's a brand new day.'
As before.

Jesus taught us all to go his way,
Get out of bed and go with him today.

Jesus showed that he can make us new,
Get out of bed and ask him what to do.

Jesus loves us all just like he said,
Get out of bed and shake your sleepy head.

God said, 'Do not be afraid'

Music: Joan Stride

God said, 'Do not be a-fraid I will help you,
Do not be a-fraid I will help you,
Do not be a-fraid Do not be a-fraid,' God said,
'Do not be a-fraid I will help you.'

God said, 'Do not be afraid, I will help you.
'Do not be afraid, I will help you.
'Do not be afraid, do not be afraid.
God said, 'Do not be afraid, I will help you.'

Y.E.S.

Music: Rose Williams

When we find the right things hard, And don't know what to do
When bad things look eas - ier, But we know that they are wrong.

Don't let us be temp - ted, Lord. We'd ra - ther fol - low you. Oh
Help us to re - mem - ber, Lord, The cho - rus of this song.

Y. E. S. Yes, dear Lord, Please show us what to do.

N. O. No! We won't do wrong, We'd ra - ther be like you.

Giving praise to God

Music: John Baker

Help - ing fin - gers and help -ing hands   Giv - ing   praise to   God.

Helping fingers and helping hands,
Giving praise to God.

Kindly fingers and kindly hands,
Giving praise to God.

Caring fingers and caring hands,
Giving praise to God.

Busy fingers and busy hands,
Giving praise to God.

This song and the next will be best used when children are learning about ways of serving God. They should be given opportunities of helping and working for others to make the songs real to them.

Talking to God

I can say to God,
'I am feeling sad.'
I can say to God,
'I am feeling glad.'
He will hear me when I say,
'I feel sad or cross today.
You know I feel this way.
Please help me, God.'

Hands to greet

Music: Joan Stride

Hands to greet and fold in prayer. Hands to bless and show your care. Hands to clap and hands to raise. Hands to show our love and praise!

Talk to God

Sing to the tune: 'All things bright and beautiful.'

Chorus:
Talk to God and share with him
The thoughts you have each day.
Let him know what's on your mind.
He loves to hear you pray.

With 'Sorry', 'Please', and 'Thank you',
There's such a lot to say.
God loves to hear you praying
At any time of day.

In any place you go to
Our Father God is there;
He knows what you are thinking,
He listens to each prayer.

Our music

Listen to the wind,
Oooo!
Listen to the rain,
Pitter, patter.
Listen to the people
Hands behind ears.
Praising God again!

Listen to the fly,
Vvv!
Listen to the bee,
Buzz!
Listen to the dog bark,
Woof!
Praising God with me!
Point to self.

Listen to us sing,
Hands behind ears.
Listen to us play,
Mime playing instruments.
Listen to us clap,
Clap.
Praising God today!

We make things with our hands

Music: C. King

We make things with our hands, we make things with our hands, to please

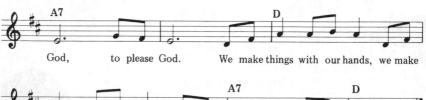

God, to please God. We make things with our hands, we make

things with our hands to please God, to please God.

We make things with our hands,
We make things with our hands,
To please God, to please God.
We make things with our hands,
We make things with our hands,
To please God, to please God.

Other verses can be made up, changing the word 'things' to 'pictures', 'models' or other things that have been made by children. In the final verse, change the words, 'To please God' to 'Thank you, God'.

Index

* indicates items which are also suitable for use with all ages together.